# The AZTECS

## Revised and Updated

JANE SHUTER

Heinemann
LIBRARY

**www.heinemann.co.uk/library**
Visit our website to find out more information about Heinemann Library books.

To order:
☎ Phone 44 (0) 1865 888066
🖹 Send a fax to 44 (0) 1865 314091
🖥 Visit the Heinemann Bookshop at www.heinemann.co.uk/library to browse our catalogue and order online.

First published in Great Britain by Heinemann, Halley Court, Jordan Hill, Oxford, OX2 8EJ, part of Harcourt Education.
Raintree is a registered trademark of Harcourt Education Ltd.

© Harcourt Education Ltd 1998, 2007
Second edition first published in paperback in 2008
The moral right of the proprietor has been asserted.

Editorial: Clare Lewis
Design: Richard Parker and Q2A Solutions
Picture Research: Hannah Taylor and
   Ruth Blair
Production: Helen McCreath

Printed and bound in China by WKT Ltd

13 digit ISBN 978 0431 07686 7 (hardback)
11 10 09 08 07
10 9 8 7 6 5 4 3 2 1

13 digit ISBN 978 0431 07743 7 (paperback)
12 11 10 09 08
10 9 8 7 6 5 4 3 2 1

**British Library Cataloguing in Publication Data**
Shuter, Jane
History Opens Windows: The Aztecs
972'.018
A full catalogue record for this book is available from the British Library.

**Acknowledgements**
The publishers would like to thank the following for permission to reproduce photographs:
Ancient Art & Architecture, p. **22**; Archivo Iconografico, S.A./Corbis, p. **10**; Bettmann/Corbis, p. **18**; Bridgeman Art Library/Biblioteca Medicea-Laurenziana, Florence, p. **6**; Bridgeman Art Library/British Library, London, p. **14**; Charles and Josette Lenars/Corbis, p. **11**; Corbis, p. **21**; Giraudon/ Art Resource, p. **26**; Michel Zabe/Art Resource, p. **27**; Mireille Vautier/The Art Archive/Antochiw Collection, Mexico p. **30**; Mireille Vautier /The Art Archive/National Archives, Mexico, p. **8**; Museum fur Volkerkunde, Vienna/Werner Forman/Art Resource, p. **9**; National Museum of Anthropology, Mexico City/Werner Forman/Art Resource, pp. **17**, **29**; Pigorini Museum of Prehistory and Ethnography, Rome/Werner Forman/Art Resource, p. **12**; Scala/Art Resource, p. **24**; The Art Archive, p. **20**; The Art Archive/Biblioteca Nacional Madrid/Dagli Orti, pp. **23**, **25**; Werner Forman/Art Resource, pp. **16**, **28**.

Illustrations, p. **30**; Eileen Mueller Neill, p. **4**; David Westerfield, pp. **7**, **13**, **15**, **19**.

Cover photograph reproduced with permission of Werner Forman Archive / Museum für Volkerkunde, Vienna.

Every effort has been made to contact copyright holders of any material reproduced in this book. Any omissions will be rectified in subsequent printings if notice is given to the publishers.

# Contents

Some words are shown in bold, **like this**.
You can find out what they mean by looking in the glossary.

# Introduction

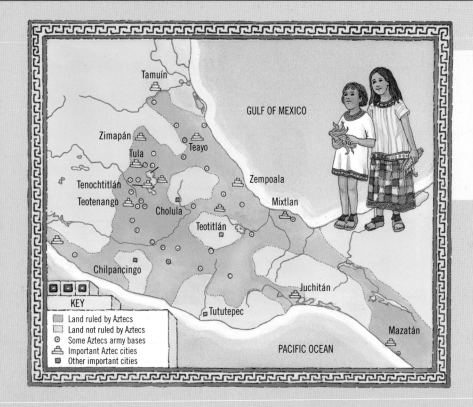

This map shows lands the Aztecs ruled in about 1500.

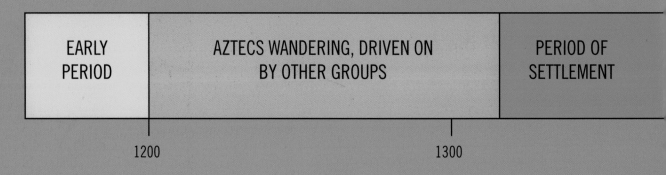

1325:
Aztecs settle in
Tenochtitlan

| EARLY PERIOD | AZTECS WANDERING, DRIVEN ON BY OTHER GROUPS | PERIOD OF SETTLEMENT |
|---|---|---|

1200         1300

The Aztecs were a group of people who became powerful in Central America starting in about 1430. They had no settled home until they built the city of Tenochtitlán on Lake Texcoco, in modern Mexico, in about 1325. From then on they became more and more powerful.

At first, the Aztecs took control of the area around Tenochtitlán. They did this by making **alliances** with other groups, such as the lords of Texcoco, who were very powerful in the area. When the Aztecs were strong enough, they began to take over by force instead. By 1500 they controlled a large part of modern Mexico. By the time the Spanish arrived in 1519, the Aztec leader, Montezuma II, ruled a rich **empire** of more than one million people.

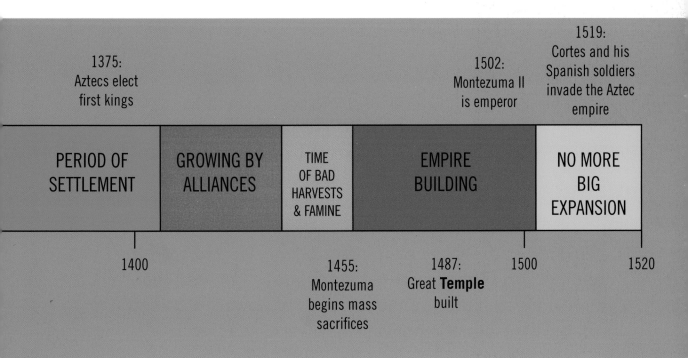

1375:
Aztecs elect
first kings

1502:
Montezuma II
is emperor

1519:
Cortes and his
Spanish soldiers
invade the Aztec
empire

| PERIOD OF SETTLEMENT | GROWING BY ALLIANCES | TIME OF BAD HARVESTS & FAMINE | EMPIRE BUILDING | NO MORE BIG EXPANSION |

1400

1455:
Montezuma
begins mass
sacrifices

1487:
Great **Temple**
built

1500

1520

# How were the Aztecs ruled?

The Aztecs had laws about crimes, property ownership, marriage, and divorce. This Aztec painting shows four judges deciding the punishments for the two criminals in the middle.

Early Aztecs lived and worked in groups of related families, called **calpulli**. Their ruler, the *tlatoani* ("he who speaks"), was chosen by a council of people from each of the *calpulli*. He made big decisions and was a war leader. But the heads of the *calpulli* ran daily life.

As the Aztec **empire** grew, the Aztecs began to organize life not in *calpulli*, but by levels of importance. The higher up the "pyramid of power" a person was, the more important they were.

The "pyramid of power"

**Emperor**

Chief advisor

Nobles

War leader

Governors

Merchants

Priests

Scribes

Craft workers

Priests/
priestesses

Farmers

Builders

Temple
workers

Workers

Slaves

# War

The Aztecs had to be good fighters to take over other groups and keep their **empire** together. When the Aztecs decided to take over another group, they gave those people three chances to join the Aztec empire. If they did not, the priests chose a good day to fight and the army attacked at dawn. Battles were fought hand-to-hand. The Aztecs usually won.

Starting at age 15, boys were trained to fight in case there was a war. There was no permanent army, but all men had to be ready to fight. **Nobles** led the army. The most important were the Eagle Knights and the Jaguar Knights.

This is a picture list of some of the **tributes** that cities in the Aztec empire had to send to Tenochtitlán. It shows some of the things the Aztecs saw as valuable.

This shield probably belonged to the ruler Ahuitzotl. The wooden back is decorated with a picture of a fierce animal.

Each **calpulli** had a storehouse for weapons and armour. The head of the *calpulli* had to make sure there were enough weapons and armour and that everything was kept in good repair.

The Aztecs fought with stone-tipped spears and clubs. They also used slings and bows with stone-tipped arrows. Their armour was made of padded cotton, soaked in salt water to stiffen it. The armour was often painted or decorated with feathers. Aztec shields were made from wood and leather, or cloth. They were often decorated.

# Religion

The Aztecs believed in many different gods and goddesses who controlled every part of life. Some were more powerful than others. All of them needed to be kept happy with prayers, music, and dancing. They also needed to be given things – food, gifts, but most of all, human blood. Without gifts of blood the gods would stop the rain, the Sun, and everything else. Often priests and other people in the city would give some of their blood in a bowl. But sometimes the gods wanted a whole life. The Aztecs believed that it was an honour to be **sacrificed**.

This carved stone head shows the Moon goddess. The circles on her cheeks are bells, because the Aztecs also called her "Lady Golden Bells".

This picture shows the modern remains of the **Temple** of the Sun, built in Teotihuacán by the Aztecs.

The Aztecs told many stories about the gods. One of these stories was about the white-skinned Feathered Serpent god, Quetzalcoatl, who had created humans. He was the only god who was against human sacrifice. He tried to stop the Aztecs from making human sacrifices. But the Aztecs thought that if they stopped, the world would end. So Quetzalcoatl sailed away, to the east. The story said that he would come back in the year Reed One, or 1519. This story would have a terrible effect when 1519 came.

# Temples and buildings

**Temples** were the homes of the gods, so they were the biggest and best decorated of all Aztec buildings. They had to be tall, reaching up to the gods in the sky. They had to be at the centre of a city, because the Aztecs had five directions: north, south, east, west, and centre. The centre was where this world joined the world of the gods and the different worlds the Aztecs believed they went to after death. So temples were built in a walled temple area in the centre of the city, with gates to the north, south, east, and west.

This is the handle of a knife that was used for sacrifices in religious **ceremonies**.

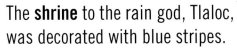

The Templo Mayor in Tenochtitlán was built for two important Aztec gods.

The **shrine** to the rain god, Tlaloc, was decorated with blue stripes.

The shrine to the war god, Huitzilopochtli, was decorated with white skulls.

The temple was in the great square in the centre of the city and was surrounded by other temples.

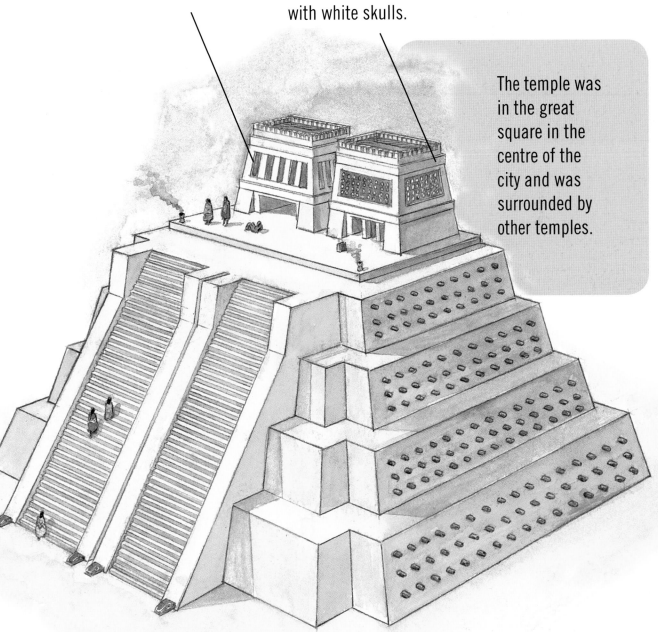

# Cities

Aztec cities were divided into different areas. The walled **temple** area was at the centre of the city. Spreading out from this area were royal palaces, homes of important **nobles**, traders' homes, and the homes and workshops of craft workers and ordinary people. These were all in different "wards", each based on *calpulli*, and run by its own officials.

The largest and most important Aztec city was Tenochtitlán. Built on Lake Texcoco, it was the first Aztec city. It grew so much that it reached Tlateloco, the other city on the lake. Both these cities had **canals** as well as roads.

This early European map of Tenochtitlán was made shortly after the Spanish invasion.

## Tenochtitlán

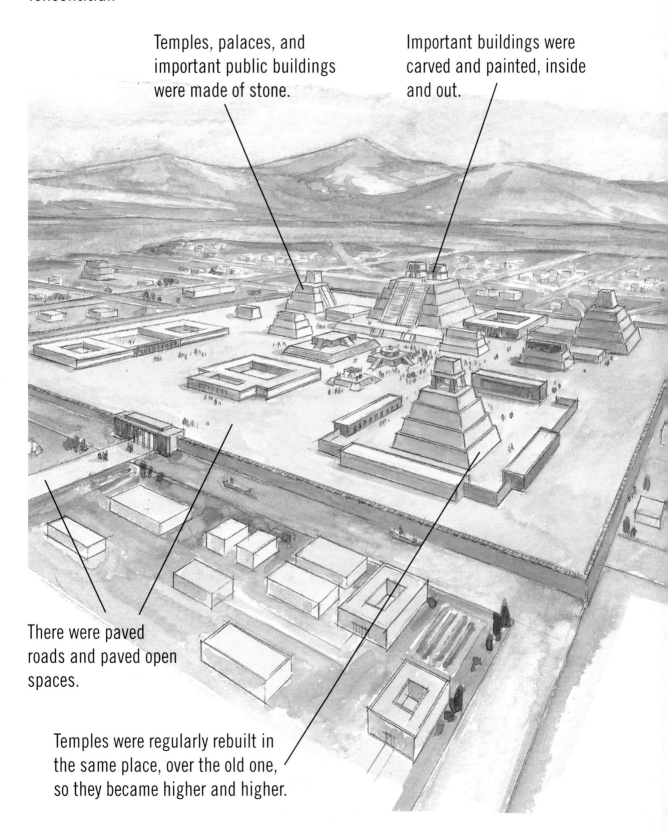

Temples, palaces, and important public buildings were made of stone.

Important buildings were carved and painted, inside and out.

There were paved roads and paved open spaces.

Temples were regularly rebuilt in the same place, over the old one, so they became higher and higher.

# Trade and travel

The Aztecs travelled on foot or in canoes. They did not ride animals or use wheeled carts. Even traders, who travelled a long way, walked if they could not travel by water. The Aztecs traded in two ways.

Ordinary people went to market and traded pots, food, or anything else they had grown or made for things they wanted.

Pochetecatl, or traders, had their own rules and levels of importance. They explored other lands for the emperor and brought back raw materials, such as precious stones, that craft workers needed. They also brought things that only the **emperor** or his **nobles** could buy.

This is a drawing of a trader, from an Aztec book. Traders had to carry everything on their backs, unless they were important enough to have a servant or slave to carry things for them.

This modern recreation shows part of a town market.

Every Aztec village, town, and city had at least one market. In large markets, everyone selling the same thing sat together. The market at Tlateloco was the biggest. All markets had the same rules. Instead of using money, the Aztecs **bartered**. They could also use cocoa beans or lengths of cloth to make up any difference in value. Breaking the rules about fair prices meant punishment in the local court.

# Food and farming

This drawing shows an Aztec farmer weeding his corn plants with a digging stick.

Aztec farmers grew corn to make flour and *atolli*, a porridge that was often flavoured with honey or chillis. They also grew chillis, peppers, beans, squash, onions, tomatoes, sweet potatoes, and cocoa beans. They kept turkeys and dogs for meat and also hunted wild animals such as deer and rabbits.

Only important people ate meat every day. Ordinary people ate more fish and seafood than meat. However, ordinary people mostly ate *atolli* and flat bread, tortillas, or tamales, wrapped around vegetables. Women did the cooking over an open fire. They cooked mostly stews or mixtures cooked in a pot on the open flames. Whole fish and meat could be roasted.

Tenochtitlán was built on a lake. The Aztecs made "land" on the lake by building *chinampas*. These were floating fields built on mats made of **reeds**. The Aztecs were skilled farmers and grew many crops in the *chinampa*.

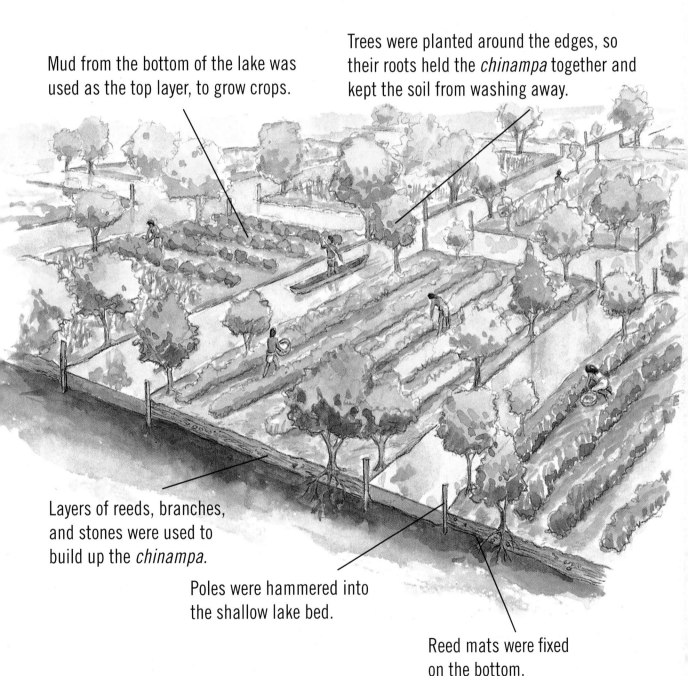

Mud from the bottom of the lake was used as the top layer, to grow crops.

Trees were planted around the edges, so their roots held the *chinampa* together and kept the soil from washing away.

Layers of reeds, branches, and stones were used to build up the *chinampa*.

Poles were hammered into the shallow lake bed.

Reed mats were fixed on the bottom.

# Families

In towns and villages, most of the *calpulli* lived in simple rectangular houses built from mud bricks with a **reed** roof. They had a door, but no windows. The floor was made of cement that was painted red and polished. There was a **hearth** for cooking and a stone for grinding corn. People sat on mats or straw cushions.

A young man married in his early twenties, usually to a younger girl. The wedding was an important occasion for the *calpulli*.

Babies were very important to the Aztecs. A woman who died in childbirth had the same funeral as a warrior killed in battle.

This picture shows a husband and wife in their home. The Aztecs believed that the husband was the most important person in the family, so he has a stool to sit on. Most people sat on mats.

This picture shows how most children were educated. A father is teaching his son how to fish, while the mother teaches her daughter how to weave.

Aztec men worked and fought while women cared for the home and the family. Children were brought up to follow their parents. Boys learned their fathers' trades, and girls learned to run a home.

Boys from important families, as well as some clever boys from ordinary families, went to one of the special schools that trained them to be priests, **scribes**, or warriors. Most boys from ordinary families went to a local school to learn how to fight. Everyone had to learn the songs and dances for religious **festivals**. The House of Song, where these were taught to children aged between 12 and 15, was the only school that girls went to.

# Clothes

Most of the Aztecs' clothes were made from cotton dyed with vegetable dyes. The clothes were made by folding and tying a piece of cloth. All men wore **loincloths**, and some of them also wore skirts. Women wore long skirts and **tunics**. Most people also wore a tilmatli – a cape tied at the shoulder.

Even though everyone wore the same style of clothes, it was easy to tell how important a person was. Priests tied their loincloths in a different way. The most important people wore the most brightly coloured, patterned, and decorated clothes.

This beautiful headdress is a copy of one that was worn by Montezuma.

This painting of Montezuma and a priest was made by a Spanish artist soon after the Spanish arrived. It shows the types of clothes that important people wore.

There were laws about what people wore. You could tell what job people did by the clothes they were wearing. Capes had the most rules. Ordinary people could not wear cotton capes. They had to wear capes made from leaf fibres from various plants. There were rules about length, colour, pattern, and even how the cape was tied.

Clothing rules also applied to shoes, hairstyles, and jewellery. For example, **nobles** wore decorated leather sandals, while ordinary people wore sandals of woven leaves.

# Entertainment

These Aztecs are playing *patolli*. This was a game where people raced bean counters around a board. Everyone could play this game.

Some Aztec sports and games were only played by one group of people. Only **nobles** could play *tlachtli*, a ball game. It was played on a long narrow court with stone walls along the long sides. Each team tried to get a rubber ball to the other team's end of the court. They could bounce it off people and the walls, but they could not let it touch the ground. The game could be won at any time by throwing the ball through stone rings on the side walls that were just big enough for the ball to go through. This game was mainly played at religious **festivals**.

Music was very important to the Aztecs. Singing, dancing, and music were part of almost all religious festivals. All children had to learn the songs and dances for the religious festivals. They were expected to join in when the festivals were held and to know just what to sing and do.

Because music was such a big part of the Aztec religion, the Spanish destroyed most Aztec musical instruments when they tried to stamp out their religion. But there are still pictures from the time to show the kinds of instruments the Aztecs played. The most important of these were drums, rattles, and pipes.

This picture shows Aztecs dancing at a religious festival. The drummers in the middle are playing two different kinds of drums.

# Writing and calendars

The Aztecs spoke a language called *Nahuatl*. They also had a written language that used pictures called glyphs. They wrote painted folding books, called codices, on paper made from tree bark. Few people could read, and even fewer could write. Some boys trained as **scribes** in special schools where they learned to draw glyphs. They had to learn many rules about colour and size.

Some glyphs were simple – for example, footprints meant travel. But many glyphs were meant to remind people of a story they had been told by showing a single, important scene from that story.

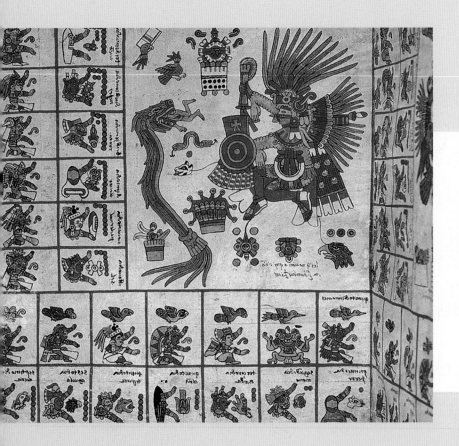

This is part of a codex – you can see the fold line on the right side of the big picture. The big picture is the "reminding" scene.

This stone shows part of the Aztec sacred calendar. The face in the centre is the Sun god.

The Aztecs had two calendars. The first was the "sacred calendar". This combined 20 names and 13 numbers in a complicated system, which repeated itself after 260 days.

The second calendar was the seasonal calendar that the Aztecs used to decide when to plant and harvest crops. It was based around the number 20 because that is how many fingers and toes a person has. It had 18 months of 20 days each, making a 360-day year. Each month had a **festival** for a particular god. The year was completed with five unlucky days, which had no name or god.

# Crafts

Jewellers like the one who made this ornament were important. The most skilled of them often worked just for the **emperor** in workshops in the emperor's palace.

To begin with, the Aztecs were self-supporting, meaning that they made or grew everything they needed. But as their **empire** grew and markets became an important part of daily life, more and more people specialized in making just one thing.

This meant that craft workers became more skilled at their trade. This could be anything from building to making pots, making jewellery or working with feathers. In cities, craft workers lived in a particular area with the other families, often from the same *calpulli*, who had the same skill.

Craft workers who made gold and silver jewellery and offerings for the gods were probably the most important of all craft workers. They worked just for the emperor, **temples**, and **nobles**. The Mixtec people, who had been taken over by the Aztecs, were the most skilful gold workers. Mixtec **tribute** was often paid mainly in gold, although other Aztec craft workers learned Mixtec techniques. It was stories of gold that led the Spanish to try to take over the Aztec empire.

This piece of gold jewellery was made by the Mixtecs. The Sun god is in the centre of the circle.

# End of the empire

metztitlan.

This Aztec picture shows a Spanish attack. With the advantage of horses and guns, the Spanish were able to beat the Aztecs.

The year 1519 was when the Aztecs believed the god Quetzalcoatl would return with an army. When the **emperor** Montezuma heard that an army had arrived, he did not know what to do. Was their leader, Hernán Cortés, a god or an enemy? Montezuma decided to greet him as a god, just in case.

By the time he realized Cortés was an enemy, it was too late. He had welcomed Cortés and his men into Tenochtitlán. He tried to get rid of the Spanish. But they had horses, cannons, guns, and help from people the Aztecs had taken over. Also, the Aztecs still fought to take prisoners, while the Spanish killed as many Aztecs as they could. By 1521 the Spanish had killed all the Aztecs or made them slaves.

# Glossary

**alliance**   agreement between groups or countries to protect and help each other

**barter**   to trade one thing for another without using money

*calpulli*   group of families who lived and worked together

**canal**   deep ditch filled with water that is used for boats or for irrigation

**ceremony**   set of actions with religious meaning

**emperor**   ruler who has total power, like a king

**empire**   group of territories or lands controlled by one country

**festival**   time of celebration with special events and entertainment

**hearth**   flat bed of stones for lighting a fire on

**loincloth**   short skirt that covers the part of the body between the waist and thighs

**noble**   important person

**reed**   tall, thick grass that grows in wet areas

**scribe**   person whose job was to read, write, and keep records

**sacrifice**   to kill an animal or human as an offering (gift) to a god

**shrine**   special place for worshipping gods or dead relatives

**temple**   building that is the home of gods and goddesses, where people pray to them

**tribute**   payment made by one ruler or group of people to another, usually to keep peace

**tunic**   garment shaped like a knee-length T-shirt

# Find out more

**Books to read**
*Hands on Ancient History: Aztecs*, Lisa Klobuchar (Heinemann Library, 2006)
*Understanding People in the Past: The Aztecs*, Rosemary Rees (Heinemann Library, 2006)

**Using the Internet**
Explore the Internet to find out more about the Aztecs. Use a search engine, such as www.yahooligans.com or www.internet4kids.com and type in a keyword or phrase such as "Montezuma" or "Tenochtitlán".

# Pronunciation guide

atolli: ah-TOLL-lee
calpulli: kal-POOL-lee
chinampa: chi-NAM-pah
Huitzilopochtli: weet-zeel-oh-POCH-tlee
Montezuma: mon-te-ZOO-mah
Nahuatl: nah-hoo-AH-tul

patolli: pah-TOLL-lee
pochetecatl: poh-che-te-KAH-tul
Quetzalcoatl: ket-zal-co-AH-tul
Tenochtitlán: ten-och-teet-LAN
tlachtli: tlach-tlee
Tlaloc: tlah-lock
tilmatli: teel-MAT-lee
tlatoani: tlah-to-AH-nee

# Index